T0065529

Hope *in* Him

Lorenzo Johnson, Jr., EdD,
Victor Small, *and*
Ralph Wilson, Jr.

WestBow Press books may be ordered through booksellers or by contacting:

WestBow Press
A Division of Thomas Nelson & Zondervan
1663 Liberty Drive
Bloomington, IN 47403
www.westbowpress.com
844-714-3454

ISBN: 978-1-6642-1867-3 (sc)
ISBN: 978-1-6642-1866-6 (hc)
ISBN: 978-1-6642-1868-0 (e)

Library of Congress Control Number: 2021900258

Print information available on the last page.

WestBow Press rev. date: 1/28/2021

Contents

Introduction

College and young adult life can be challenging. Young adults spend their lives trying to balance academic life, social life, work life, and personal life' and sometimes this can become overwhelming. Life has its share of challenges and hardships. Often, these can often be difficult to navigate without the voice of assistance or help from others who have been in similar situations.

This 31 Day Devotional Guide is designed for the active young adult on the go. Its purpose is to assist young men and women everywhere in discovering who they are in Christ Jesus and provide daily "destiny work" for them to think about while they take the steps to reach their God-given destiny.

A Letter With You In Mind

Dear Young Reader,

Thank you for taking the time to read thus far one of the most critical supplemental books that can positively impact your Christian life. As you go through these devotionals, remember to ask God for wisdom and understanding so that your mind will receive the spiritual illumination of the Word of God.

Remember, God did not design hell for His children. He created hell for the devil and his angels. Due to the innate lust of humanity, and our continued disobedience to the Word of God, hell enlarges herself daily (*King James Version*, Isaiah 5:14). So, this answers the question that humans can go to hell if they choose. But how can one get to Heaven? What if a person is a good person? They give to the poor, volunteer their time, go to church every Sunday and live a clean lifestyle. Will they go to Heaven? The answer to this question is no.

God came to this earth in the likeness of Jesus Christ to redeem man and give him a chance to have eternal life with Christ. There isn't one person created that God wouldn't want to see accept His salvation, become filled with His spirit (Holy Ghost), and live for Him. For the Bible says, "He is not willing that any should perish but that all come unto repentance" (*King James Version*, 2 Peter 2:9). So, one (we) must first repent of their sins, no matter how "good" we are.

After we repent of our sins, what do we do next? The Apostle Paul in the book of Acts tells us to repent and be baptized in the name of the Lord Jesus for the remission of our sins and ye shall receive the gift of the Holy Ghost. God made us a promise. For the promise is unto us and our children and to as many as a far off. Christ made the plan of salvation available to and for us (*King James Version*, Acts 2:38-39).

So how do we receive the Holy Ghost? Well, once you repent (acknowledge your sins and vow to turn away from them) and accept Christ in your life, He gives you the Holy Ghost according to Acts 2:38 (KJV). At that moment, He gives you the access code to the realm of power, but just like a bank card or credit card you receive in the mail. But you must first call to activate its usage and power. If you never call the bank or credit card company, the card won't be activated and you won't receive the benefits of the card, neither will you enjoy the power of its spending. This credit card reference is a very shallow example but I'm trying to paint a picture through a shared and familiar experience. If you do not call on the Lord with your whole heart after you have accepted Him into your life, and humble yourself so that you only want Him, then you won't unlock the benefits of the power (Holy Ghost) that is within you. The Bible says if you humble yourself under the mighty hand of God, He will exalt you in due time (*King James Version*, I Peter 5:6). If you pray sincerely and focus on Him, He will validate your access and provide you with the operation of the Holy Spirit in your life.

It is with this great power of the Holy Ghost that we can heal the sick, raise the dead, and cast out demons. Jesus did it, and He told us in His Word that greater works shall we do (*King James Version*, John 14:12). And He can't lie, for God is not a man that He should lie neither the son of man that He should repent (*King James Version*, Numbers 23:19). And before His Word returns back void in His mouth, He said Heaven and Earth would pass away (*King James Version*, Matthew 24:5).

No human is able to defeat the powers of the enemy alone. And it takes a person who is saved and filled with the power of God to speak those things that be not as though they were;

and bind and loose those things in the earth, as they will be bound and loosed in Heaven. After you have been filled with the Holy Ghost, you will be a threat to the enemy. He will bring out the "big guns" on you. You might experience more stress from school, family, relationships or you may experience an influx of people in your circle with temptation. Remember the He will twist what God says and what you see to make you doubt God. So, whatever it is, get ready for it. But know Christ said he would never leave you nor forsake you. He said in His Word that you are more than a conqueror (*King James Version*, Romans 8:37). No matter how you view your circumstances, when the devils comes against you, the Bible says count it all joy (*King James Version,* James 1:2). For we know we walk by faith and not by sight (*King James Version*, II Corinthians 5:7). So even if you don't see the victory, continue to claim it because it's already done. It is with this kind of faith that God moves. You don't need much faith; only the size of a mustard seed will move or change your situation (*King James Version*, Matthew 17:20). Then and only then will you have the power to speak to the mountain and cause it to move (*King James Version*, Mark 11:22-24).

You don't have to be on an altar in church to receive the Holy Ghost. You can be at home, in your car, on your job or walking down the street. Location does not matter, but the condition of your heart does. If your heart is filled with pride, you won't receive access until you get rid of pride. If your heart is filled with the lust of the flesh, wicked perversion, and unforgiveness of others; the access will be denied until you release those things.

Don't get caught up in the things of this world. For the Bible teaches us that we are in the world, but not of it (*King James Version*, John 15:19). That means we have a home to go to after this life. Why live this life in misery or in mediocrity when God wants to give you the access code the devil can't crack.

Many of you have taken the first step to come to Christ through repenting of your sins and getting baptized in Jesus name according to Acts 2:38 (KJV). There is one more step that will unlock your destiny and cause the very demons of hell to submit to the authority of Christ that worketh in you, and that is receiving the power of the Holy Ghost being operational (speaking in your heavenly language) in your life (*King James Version*, Acts 1:8).

Why don't you ask God to fill you today? He is ready and willing to do it. All it takes is a submissive heart and a humble spirit. Let Him give you power today.

God Bless

DAY

1

Change Your Perspective

Scripture: "And be not conformed to this world, but be transformed by the renewing of your mind, so that you may prove what the will of God is, that which is good and acceptable and perfect" (*New American Standard Bible (NASB)*, Romans 12:2).

Lesson: One of the biggest problems that seemed to plague me in college and afterwards was the inability to see things from a different perspective. The facts and the current visuals all played a more important role than the "faith" behind what I should have been seeing. I quickly realized that if you go through life always looking at what is, instead of looking at what could be, you will always fall short of your victory.

Sometimes it's a good idea to talk to others about different situations to get their opinion(s) of what you can do. However, be careful because not everyone understands perspective, and not everyone is operating from a standpoint in your best interest. Spend some time in prayer before God, asking Him to guide your decisions and open your understanding so that you will be able to change your perspective.

Destiny Work:

- ❐ Today, focus on changing your outlook. Look at a problem or a difficult situation you are facing and look at it through the lens of Christ.
- ❐ How would Christ deal with this situation? Remember, the same power that raised Jesus from the dead is now dwelling/residing in you (KJV, Romans 6:10-11). It's time to activate your power today!

DAY

2

Your Name Carries Weight

Scripture: "A good name is rather to be chosen than great riches, and loving favor rather than silver and gold" (*King James Version*, Proverbs 22:1).

Lesson: The Rockefellers, Fendi, Gucci, and Tom Ford; yup, chances are you have heard at least one, if not all of those names. When we tend to think of other popular names, famous people like Idris Elba, Michael Jordan, Cardi B, Jay-Z and others pop in our heads. Very rarely do we think of our own personal names.

Our names were given to us at birth by our parents, or by someone who loved us. Those names represent who we are. Oftentimes as we grow, we begin to look at others and begin to envy how they are living, how they are being social online and attracting fans, or how they are partying on a weekly basis; seeming to be living the good life with no worries. We look at our lives and begin to compare them to others. Although we may have had some challenging life experiences growing up, and although we may have endured and conquered great hardships, we still belittle our lives because it isn't glamorized on social media or spread abroad on some platform for the world to see.

Did you ever stop to think that maybe those people who seem to be living the good life and having all this fun, are actually hurting inside? Did you ever stop to wonder if they are over compensating for their weaknesses or lack of commitment to their family; not to mention are you aware of how many prescription medications many of these people are using just to make it through the day or night? This message is for someone out there who is struggling with their name; and when I say "name" I mean your life; because your name is all you have… it is your life. Don't lose sight of who you are due to what others are doing. You were put here for a reason. Find out that purpose and stick to your passion and vision. When you find your purpose, passion, and vision, then no one will be able to sucker you in to buying a dream or a reality that wasn't meant for you.

Destiny Work:

❒ Don't ruin your name just because you can't find your way, or see a way out. Look up and focus on Christ;

that way you won't be distracted but He will guide you to your ordered steps.

- ❒ Call someone who you really know is rooted in the Word of God and that will give you non biased, non-judgmental advice. Build a working relationship with this person so that you are able to reach out to him/her on a consistent basis for advice and a thought partner. We all need someone to hold us accountable because not only is our name on the line, but God's name is too. God is the manufacturer of our lives and He doesn't make junk.
- ❒ If you give your life to the one who created you, He will help you fix what you can't see so that you understand who you are.

DAY

3

Operate in Silence

Scripture: The story of a shepherd boy named Joseph (*KJV*, Genesis 37).

Lesson: In the above scripture, we find that Joseph was favored by God and he had big dreams. He told those dreams to people who were closest to him, such as his friends and his own brothers. Due to those around him being jealous of his dreams, he was sold into slavery by his older brothers, simply because they were jealous and envious of what God has placed inside of Joseph-- and that was a vision of greatness.

When you share your visions and dreams with people who have no concrete vision or dreams, you become the victim. There are dream killers in this world who have an evil assignment by the enemy to destroy your life. Oftentimes, they become closer to us than we think. They appear to befriend us and have our backs but they blind us and ultimately leave us lonely and hopeless. They create manipulating situations and put us in predicaments that might cause us to mentally wrestle with our decision and the scope of our lives. As the United Negro College Fund puts it, "a mind is a terrible thing to waste"; and if the enemy can steal your mind, your thoughts, and your peace, then you are no good to anyone-- not even yourself.

Destiny Work:

- Think of some visions and dreams you had when you were younger.
- Write them all down. [I would dare say rank them in order of your passion]. Are you still interested in pursuing them? If so, put together a logical plan of action with steps that are attainable.
- Remember, it may be tempting to tell people about this vision, as you are excited and you want others to be as well; but the bottom line is to operate in silence. I'm not saying you shouldn't tell someone, but the more people you speak to about this, the more conversation and differences of opinions you may get. Having too many differences of opinions could place these visions and dreams back on the shelf for another few years, or forever-- simply because someone else didn't believe in your vision because they never had one.

DAY

4

Favor over Beauty

Scripture: The story of Esther and her rise to favor (*KJV*, The Book of Esther).

Lesson: The above Book of Esther is a very short book in the Old Testament. It has ten short chapters but it is filled with some amazing elements. The Book of Esther talks about a beautiful queen named Vashti who was initially married to King Ahasuerus. King Ahasuerus was a rich and powerful ruler, and he wanted to show his queen off in front of everyone. One day he summoned Vashti to come unto him so that he could show her off in front of his throne. She denied the request because she didn't feel like being the center of attention. This refusal made the King upset and he had Vashti thrown out of his kingdom.

The King needed a new queen and he found her in a most unique way. She was basically a peasant girl who was brought to the palace. I won't ruin it for you but long story short, the peasant girl named Esther had a very humble and beautiful spirit. And her beauty from within began to show outwardly on her countenance when she spoke and when she graced the presence of the king. You see, Esther eventually found favor in the site of her husband the king. Because she wasn't prideful but obedient, she always respected the king, no matter how wrong he was; therefore, she always managed to find favor in his site.

Many of you have heard the anonymous phrase "favor ain't fair". And that is true. The favor of God is something that only God can give us, and nothing we can earn. When His favor is upon us, all things are even more possible because it provides us direct access to the things we want, need, and even don't qualify for. Esther, a peasant girl who had no family and was raised by a family friend, would have never been a queen if one would go off qualifications. She wasn't royal and neither had she land and cattle to leverage as money. But one thing she did have that moved her to the front of the line was the favor of God.

Destiny Work:

- ❐ There may be some areas in your life or situations you are about to face that may not be in your favor. You may be applying to medical school but don't have the grades, application fees, nor the patient care hours to be a viable candidate. You may be a financially broke college student who can't seem to manage their finances, find the funding to pay for school, not to mention may not even be on track to graduate. You might even be a two-time convicted felon about to be placed on lockdown for the next few years. Whatever your situation or dilemma, the favor of God can turn things around for you.

- ❒ Now, favor is not just going to be given to you haphazardly, neither can it be earned through you merits alone. Well, how can you obtain favor you ask?
- ❒ You just have to ask God earnestly for His favor to cover you and your situation. If you believe with all your heart and don't doubt, God will grant you His favor and change your situation. Just remember, you can't fool God. He really knows your heart. So, you must be sincere and willing to put away those things that are blocking your relationship with Him. Go to Him. Be sincere. Experience His favor.

DAY

5

Trust Your Instinct

Scripture: "Ye shall receive power after that the Holy Ghost is come upon you: and ye shall be witnesses unto me both in Jerusalem, and in all Judaea, and in Samaria, and unto the uttermost part of the earth" (*KJV,* Acts 1:8).

Lesson: You ever get the feeling sometimes that a decision you made just wasn't the right one. I mean, it's like you knew before you chose that you weren't choosing the right thing. Like that guy or girl you met at the club who was looking really cute. You all started to talk and you felt that immediate attraction. A few days later as you continue talking, you find out that their life and lifestyle is a little different from what you are accustomed to. I mean you really know their life is jacked up and they don't really seem to care about the things that matter in life; just that next dose of happiness and the next good feeling. No biggie, right? So, you continue to converse with them and become more deeply involved; intimate even. You then start to really wonder if you've made the right decision about aligning yourself and your vision with this person. But you don't act on it because this person really knows how to emotionally make you feel good, and they make you feel like it's you and them against the world. You have these awful gut punches that continue to hit you when they call or text, when they talk to you, or when you are near them. But time and time again you ignore the punches. That my friend is your instinct talking and it is signaling/warning you that danger is lurking ahead if you continue.

Our bodies give us this unique warning sign that danger is near because it knows we need to take a different course of action; a course correction if you will. Sometimes we acknowledge the warning, other times we do not. Often we try to drown out the warning with our emotions or with other things that become addictive like smoking, drinking, drugs, or sex... When you accept Christ into your life as your personal savior, He gives you a gut checker known as the Holy Ghost. The Holy Ghost's job is to comfort you and to ensure that you are always in a position to hear from God and to be led by him daily.

Whenever we ignore our instinct, we are ignoring God. He knows what is best for us, even when we feel at times, we think we know better than God. God knows that the enemy desires to destroy us, so He has given us the Holy Ghost as our guide and protector. We must trust the leading of the Holy Spirit. We must stay in His Word daily and continue to go to God in prayer. This is the only way we will be able to acknowledge the presence of the operation of the Holy Spirit in our lives.

Destiny Work:

- ❒ I want you to think about something you've committed yourself too, a relationship perhaps, or a new job.
- ❒ Did you ever get the feeling deep down that something wasn't right? Well, if so, don't ignore it.
- ❒ Think about what caused that reaction and confront it. It could be the Holy Spirit telling you there is danger ahead. Stop for a moment and check your gut. It holds more than just food; it holds your spiritual life.

DAY

6

Guiding Principles

Scripture: "Then the Lord God took the man and put him into the garden of Eden to cultivate it and keep it. The Lord God commanded the man, saying, "From any tree of the garden you may eat freely; but from the tree of the knowledge of good and evil you shall not eat, for in the day that you eat from it you will surely die" (*NASB*, Genesis 2:15-17).

Lesson: God's seemingly simple command to Adam was to eat of every tree of the garden, *EXCEPT* for the tree of knowledge of good and evil. Although this one restriction was a moral test, it reveals to us that God has always expected our obedience and acceptance of His Word. Faith and obedience are the principles which govern our relationship with God, as it did with Adam in the Garden of Eden. God warned Adam that if he disobeyed His will, he would surely die. The challenge for Adam was to trust God's command because he hadn't yet known the reality of human death. Death was a foreign term to Adam because he had access to the tree of life, which secured an eternal existence. If Adam had the faith to believe beyond his experience, then God's command would have assuredly produced his obedience.

On the flip side, an eternal existence in God's presence is difficult for our minds to conceive because we have yet to experience immortality. But I assure you it's attainable. If we follow God's command, then we too shall have a right to the tree of life and may enter in through the gates into the city (*KJV*, Revelation 22:14).

Destiny Work:

- ❒ In life, we have a choice: to either obey God's Word and have abundant life, or rebel and choose eternal damnation (separation from God's presence). This is a definite choice. There's no in between. The Apostle Peter tells us that the righteous or those that are morally excellent, shall scarcely be saved (*KJV*, I Peter 4:18).
- ❒ So, what does this mean for an unrepentant sinner or a fence straddler? By no means are any of us perfect, but each of us must be intentional in our choice to obey God and live a life pleasing unto Him. What's your choice?

DAY

7

My Boundaries

Scripture: "And you were dead in your trespasses and sins, in which you formerly walked according to the course of this world, according to the prince of the power of the air, of the spirit that is now working in the sons of disobedience" (*NASB*, Ephesians 2:1-2).

Lesson: Verse 2 picks up, "in which you ***FORMERLY*** walked", the "you" that once walked was the old man, which after baptism in the name of Jesus, is crucified and buried. And though the buried old nature is the symptom and effect of Adam's fall from the direct presence of the Lord, we understand the influence of such (sin) lives on in our flesh. The guidance of which, being the prince of the power of the air, must be shut down or disengaged by the believer. Understanding yourself and your own triggers can inform you on what and how to abstain from certain relapses. Easier said: you know yourself better than anyone else, what causes you to be tempted and what causes you to fall victim to the enemy's influences. So, if you like sweets and are on a diet, then don't go out and get those "hot" doughnuts from your favorite bakery, neither should you probably binge watch that favorite cake show on your local cable channel. Be honest with yourself and set boundaries, as to not entice and encourage the resurrection of the former man that once took up residence in your body.

Destiny Work:

- ❒ For some of us and some of our temptations, it may take us years of building up the strength to abstain before we can again visit certain places or even be around certain people without being tempted to the point of falling. That's okay! Let's be wise enough not to put ourselves in positions of weakness, in which we have less of a chance of victory!
- ❒ God has given you victory, so walk in it!

DAY

8

All or Nothing

Scripture: "Then a scribe came and said to Him, "Teacher, I will follow You wherever You go." Jesus said to him, "The foxes have holes and the birds of the air *have* nests, but the Son of Man has nowhere to lay His head." Another of the disciples said to Him, "Lord, permit me first to go and bury my father." But Jesus said to him, "Follow Me, and allow the dead to bury their own dead" (*NASB*, Matthew 8:19-22).

Lesson: In my first in-seat seminary lecture, I met an Asian classmate who started life in China as an atheist. It wasn't until after moving to the States as a teenager that she was introduced to the Bible. After reading the scriptures, she immediately found the Word of God harmonized with her heart and she began following Jesus. She was studying to become an aerospace engineer, but after reading the scriptures, decided to give up her career to move to North Carolina and attend seminary at a local seminary and study the Word more intently full time.

In the above passage, the disciple provides a good excuse, yet Jesus says, "let the dead bury the dead". In other words, let those who are decaying and dying, spiritually, make excuses but come with me if you want to plug into the life-giving source.

Destiny Work:

- ❑ In most of the circles we run in, this sort of sacrifice is rare. Unlike my classmate, who walked away from a lucrative career, most of us prioritize careers, relationships, and possessions, rather than following Christ.
- ❑ By no means do I recommend anyone quit school or leave their job - unless explicitly instructed by the Lord - but I do invite you to sacrificially give God more of yourself today. God continues to extend an invitation to connect and reconnect with Him daily.
- ❑ What will you offer the Lord for all He has done for you? (*KJV*, Psalm 116:12)

DAY

9

Culture Changer

Scripture: "Now Simon's mother-in-law was lying sick with a fever; and immediately they spoke to Jesus about her. And He came to her and raised her up, taking her by the hand, and the fever left her, and she waited on them. When evening came, after the sun had set, they *began* bringing to Him all who were ill and those who were demon-possessed. And the whole city had gathered at the door. And He healed many who were ill with various diseases, and cast out many demons; and He was not permitting the demons to speak, because they knew who He was. In the early morning, while it was still dark, Jesus got up, left *the house*, and went away to a secluded place, and was praying there" (*NASB* Mark 1: 30-35)

Lesson: At the start of Jesus' ministry, the people were astonished by His teaching. As He healed and performed miracles, the size of His audience grew. Sure, the crowds initially came to witness the miraculous demonstrations, but as their natural needs were met their attention shifted to Christ's teaching. The old adage, people don't care what you know until they know that you care, is exactly it!

We as the church, must shift our efforts from attractive programming and music, to applying our focus to touching the needs of our neighbors. We must be strategic as we can't meet every need. However, we must leverage the resources we have access to, for guidance as to where we can initially be most impactful. There's no more time for egos, hidden agendas, nor self-promotion--it's about souls, souls, and more souls.

Destiny Work:

- ❒ Today, begin looking around your local community for opportunities to be the hands and feet of Jesus. There's a need you are equipped to meet to help change the community and culture around you.
- ❒ Find that need and love on people by fulfilling the void. If you are unsure, ask God to direct your steps and put your hands to work. The opportunity will appear. Watch out!

DAY

10

Emotional Issues

Scripture: "Because of the surpassing greatness of the revelations, for this reason, to keep me from exalting myself, there was given me a thorn in the flesh, a messenger of Satan to torment me—to keep me from exalting myself! (8) Concerning this I implored the Lord three times that it might leave me. (9) And He has said to me, "My grace is sufficient for you, for power is perfected in weakness." Most gladly, therefore, I will rather boast about my weaknesses, so that the power of Christ may dwell in me" (*NASB*, 2 Corinthians 12:7-9)

Lesson: Since the beginning of creation, humans have wrestled with and oftentimes explored the grips of defeat in the face of disappointment. The above passage conveys that Paul had some sort of thorn (opposition or inward hindrance) or something which frustrated and caused trouble in his life. Although he had experienced the power of God and had been delivered multiple times from the clutches of death, the thorn wasn't removed. Talk about being disappointed! Even though he was an apostle of Jesus Christ, he was still human just like all of us; and I'm sure felt sadness and displeasure by the nonfulfillment of his expectations. If you've lived long enough, you have also experienced this at some point or another because for whatever reason your life doesn't sometimes align with your expectations. Your high school or college classes are not going as well as you thought, and therefore feel frustrated and underwhelmed. Financially, you're struggling to make ends meet; working two jobs or unemployed and looking for work. You're not married and you seem to be meeting all the wrong people to date. At some point in your life, you may feel dissatisfied with life. What's your response to it?

Destiny Work:

- ❒ For so many, this was the point that the pressure overwhelmed them and caused them to give up. They stopped believing and lost all hope that things would turn around. But Paul continued seeking the Lord because He promised if he would seek, he would find the answer. Christ responded to the answer to Paul's question with, "my GRACE is sufficient for you"(*NASB*, 2 Corinthians 12:9).

- ❒ What God is trying to tell us is that His ability to provide us joy, pleasure, and delight in the midst of our emotional challenges is all we need. Simple as that. It's His decision whether to remove the load or to strengthen your shoulders to carry the load. Regardless, His grace is sufficient!!! Today, your challenge is to rest in God's grace.

DAY

11

Being Real in Pain

Scripture: "[2] Grace to you and peace from God our Father and the Lord Jesus Christ... [13]so that my imprisonment in *the cause of* Christ has become well known throughout the whole praetorian guard and to everyone else, [14] and that most of the brethren, trusting in the Lord because of my imprisonment, have far more courage to speak the word of God without fear" (*NASB*, Philippians 2:12-14)

Lesson: The Apostle Paul exudes his joy of the tribulations he has endured, as they have propelled the confidence in other believers to endure and continue fighting the good fight. This speaks to me because so many of us disguise our tribulations, as if life is a bed of roses for us. We get on social media and highlight the positives of our lives, we post fancy pictures and make videos that showcase the good points in our lives. We pretend to have it all and then sarcastically scorn others for not being on our "level". We understand this has a negative impact on us, but we continue the façade. However, we honestly don't think about how detrimental this is to those around us who are seeing hope and genuine validation and can't find it.

We're struggling and our faith waivers from time to time, but we put on a good face and step into our "phone booths" like George Reeves did during 1950's television show *The Adventures of Superman*, to put on our "super Christian" disguises. What we don't realize is someone, who is experiencing similar struggles, is fading...not necessarily because the condition is getting the best of them, but because they can't live up to the facade you have on display. They contemplate why you don't ever seem to struggle with anything, and if so, then "what's wrong with me?" But we see in these scriptures, how the people witnessing Paul's perseverance through persecution, emboldens them to continue to fight. They not only witness it, but he (Paul) writes about it throughout the Pauline letters [Paul's written letters to churches], as a method to encourage fellow believers to press through hardships and realize problems are also a part of this life too.

Destiny Work:

- ❒ Let us follow Paul's example and be real/transparent with those who are watching and looking to us as examples, so that they may grow and flourish in the richness of the Holy Spirit!

DAY

12

Childhood Trauma: Abandoned and Unwanted

Scripture: "Let your conversation be without covetousness; and be content with such things as ye have: for he hath said, I will never leave thee, nor forsake thee" (*KJV*, Hebrews 13:5).

Lesson: There are situations and experiences in life that we go through that leave us happy, and some that leave us empty and sad. There are some experiences that make us feel like we are accepted and loved, and there are others that come to make us feel manipulated and rejected. Things happen in life for a reason and we, oftentimes, do not get to pick when and where they happen. What we can control is how we view the situation, our response to it, and what we choose to hold on to.

Letting go of a hurtful situation can be extremely difficult. Even for strong Christians who pray and read the Word of God daily, they still may need additional support from friends, family, and mental health counselors to help them deal with the issue. And this is perfectly fine! There is nothing wrong with this at all. God has placed people in our lives, and professionally licensed people in our community to help us overcome certain challenges life presents. So, don't ever feel embarrassed or ashamed for receiving these supports. Feeling unwanted, unloved and abandoned are hurtful feelings to endure alone, and should never be kept inside. However, if we allow the Word of God to become operational and alive in our lives, as well as continue to be around people who support us, we will find the strength to realize that the situation could not break us, but it drew us closer to the love of God. You see, humans are capable of love and hurt, however God is the author of love. And it is His desire that each human reaches out to Him so He can show you this love. His love isn't emotional, although at times it will impact your emotions, but His love is called the Agape love. His love is without limits or emotions, because His love is pure. And no matter how bad you feel or how much you mess up in life, His love remains the same, unchanged.

So, whatever you are going through, or whatever you've done let it be finished at the cross. Remember, He got up so you could live. So, if you are struggling, you don't have to. Worried, confused, angered-- you don't have to be. Meet Jesus at the cross and He will show you how He has already taken care of your needs. It is there hanging on the cross, and He has given you the victory to obtain. All you have to do is continue to raise the victory banner and keep proclaiming victory until He returns again.

Destiny Work:

- ❒ As you openly reflect on your life, think about a situation and the people who placed you in a position to feel abandoned and unwanted. Are these feelings still holding you down now? If so, you must openly address this situation with the person/people to find out their intentions. Often people speak out of anger and they don't mean what they say. Find out if they really meant to place you in a situation to make you feel abandoned or unwanted.
- ❒ Next take it to the cross in prayer. After you have made your peace with the situation, give the situation entirely to Jesus and believe His Word that He will never leave you or forsake you. Even when we are hurting and can't see the silver lining, Jesus is there waiting with his arms extended for us to run to him so He can comfort us and alleviate our fears and doubts.

DAY

13

Decisions vs Consequences

Scripture: "[2] And the woman said unto the serpent, we may eat of the fruit of the trees of the garden: [3]But of the fruit of the tree which is in the midst of the garden, God hath said, Ye shall not eat of it, neither shall ye touch it, lest ye die. [4]And the serpent said unto the woman, Ye shall not surely die: [5]For God doth know that in the day ye eat thereof, then your eyes shall be opened, and ye shall be as gods, knowing good and evil. [6]And when the woman saw that the tree was good for food, and that it was pleasant to the eyes, and a tree to be desired to make one wise, she took of the fruit thereof, and did eat, and gave also unto her husband with her; and he did eat. [7]And the eyes of them both were opened, and they knew that they were naked; and they sewed fig leaves together, and made themselves aprons.

[14] And the Lord God said unto the serpent, Because thou hast done this, thou art cursed above all cattle, and above every beast of the field; upon thy belly shalt thou go, and dust

shalt thou eat all the days of thy life: [15]And I will put enmity between thee and the woman, and between thy seed and her seed; it shall bruise thy head, and thou shalt bruise his heel. [16]Unto the woman he said, I will greatly multiply thy sorrow and thy conception; in sorrow thou shalt bring forth children; and thy desire shall be to thy husband, and he shall rule over thee. [17] And unto Adam he said, Because thou hast hearkened unto the voice of thy wife, and hast eaten of the tree, of which I commanded thee, saying, Thou shalt not eat of it: cursed is the ground for thy sake; in sorrow shalt thou eat of it all the days of thy life; [18]Thorns also and thistles shall it bring forth to thee; and thou shalt eat the herb of the field; [19] In the sweat of thy face shalt thou eat bread, till thou return unto the ground; for out of it wast thou taken: for dust thou art, and unto dust shalt thou return" (*KJV*, Genesis 3:2-7; 14-19)

Lesson: In reading the above story of Adam and Eve, we see that they lived in the Garden of Eden and they basically had everything they needed. They were always in the presence of the Lord, they had all the food they could consume, and they were free from fear, hurt, and pain. There was one thing they were not supposed to do; and that was to eat of the tree of the knowledge of good and evil. See, God never wanted them to know evil. He only wanted them to know Him. However, they were both deceived by the serpent and so they ate of the tree and disobeyed God. Because of their quick decision to eat of the forbidden tree, we now are faced with eternal hardships known as their consequences.

We all have major and minor decisions to make on a daily basis. Sometimes we get so caught up in the details of making the decisions until we don't completely think about the details of the consequences. Sure, I can go out and purchase a nice car today because I have a good job, however, am I prepared to pay a monthly car payment and insurance and keep up the maintenance on it? That outfit sure looked good at the store, and those new Air Force 1 sneakers would look really nice on my feet. I have the money to pay for them, but after I get them, how will I pay my bills next week, how will I eat next week, and is this purchase a really necessary expense?

Destiny Work:

- ❒ Taking note of the consequences or effects of our decisions can add an entirely different level to our choices and in making decisions.
- ❒ Today, write down some decisions you have to make this week.
- ❒ Then write down the consequences for each decision. Make sure you can live with the consequences of the decision before you decide.

DAY

14

Change is Good. Don't Settle for Average.

Scripture: "Ye are of God, little children, and have overcome them: because greater is he that is in me, than he that is in the world" (*KJV*, I John 4:4).

Lesson: I've met a few "young people" in my lifetime that came up in nontraditional family settings. Some grew up being reared by their grandparents, some with their aunts, and others grew up with multiple family relatives throughout their lives. Many of which had either been through foster care, adoption, or were raised by people other than their biological parents. Sometimes, especially depending on the age it occurred, this may have a negative impact on the way these children see themselves in the world as they grow and mature into young adults. Many may feel they aren't good enough and struggle with emotional acceptance within relationships, while others may still ponder the question of "why did it have to happen to me" and "why didn't they want me"?

If this is you, remember you were not born into an average situation, unlike many children. You triumphed through a difficult one. One that would have caused someone else to perish if they had to walk in your shoes. You have to stop living an average life and settling for average. You were not meant to be average because God didn't create you that way. Average is doing what everyone else is doing around you. Average is not propelling yourself to move forward with your dreams or career. Average is finding yourself always participating and doing the same things in the same way-- never growing but being stagnant and always in some type of dilemma. If you need a reminder, look back on your life and see who much you have accomplished thus far. Live the way God designed for you to and failure won't be an option that hurdles your success.

Destiny Work:

- ❐ Look over your life and decisions you've made recently. Are there any areas where you are cheating yourself and settling? If so, make a plan to change this. Your future self will thank you for it.

DAY

15

I am in Christ. Christ is in Me.

Scripture: "And if you belong to Christ, then you are Abraham's descendants, heirs according to promise" (*NASB*, Galatians 3:29).

Lesson: In today's society, so many people struggle with identity issues. Many people don't understand who they really are, or what their purpose is in life. They lead their lives based on others and get caught in an identity crisis. I think an identity crisis can be defined as a period of uncertainty and confusion in which a person's sense of identity becomes insecure, or flawed; primarily due to a change in their expected ideals or position in life.

In Apostle Paul's day, some Jewish Christians instructed the newly converted Galatian (Gentile) Christians, in order to share in the covenant God made with Abraham, they would need to comply with the law and be circumcised. Here, the Apostle rejects the notion and informs the Galatians, removing the burden of the law - that in Christ they are sons and daughters of God. Though 601 of the 613 laws of the Old Testament do not necessarily apply to believers of the new covenant, as believers we can know who we are and trace our spiritual bloodlines back through the rich history of God's chosen people, as well as look forward to the ultimate promise yet to be revealed.

Destiny Work:

- ❒ Today, your challenge is looking beyond the eyes of society and fully grasping you are much more than your status nor whatever side of the tracks you grew up on. You are God's son/daughter, you are the beloved, and you are heirs with a blessed inheritance.

DAY

16

No One Knows My Pain

Scripture: "Jesus wept" (*NASB*, John 11:35).

Lesson: "Jesus wept" is the shortest verse in the Bible, but this scripture is illuminating. A funeral was the backdrop of this scripture. One of Jesus' best friends, Lazarus had died. How did he die? Well, you just have to read it for yourself because I don't want to spoil it for you.

This display of emotions by the savior of the universe reassures us that He (Jesus) fully comprehends our pain. Whether physical, mental or emotional, Jesus is acquainted with it. Newsflash!! There are no *super* Christians. We feel, we hurt, we get disappointed, and we fail; but through our human experience is woven a silver line of love. Listen to how Isaiah the prophet describes Christ: "He was despised and rejected by mankind, a man of suffering, and familiar with pain. Like one from whom people hide their faces he was despised, and we held him in low esteem" (*NASB*, Isaiah 53:3). Satan, our enemy wants you to believe that you are alone in your pain. Remember he is a liar and the father of lies (*NASB*, John 8:44).

There is a simple formula I use when dealing with painful situations. Don't nurse it, don't rehearse it, don't curse it. Pain has a ministry in the life of the believer. Pain creates an atmosphere of intimacy. The hurtful feeling of pain alone can cause us to nurse the hurt, rehearse it by talking to others and eventually curse it without ever experiencing the victory of overcoming it. We must understand that pain has purpose and ultimately pain matures us as believers and establishes our testimony. Remember to call on the name of the Lord in the midst of your pain, invite the Savior into the circumstance and watch how He gets the glory and you will be declared the victor in Jesus name.

Destiny Work:

- ❐ Pain has purpose. What lesson have you learned from painful situations? How did God get the glory?
- ❐ Write a letter to your future self-encouraging yourself in the Lord.
- ❐ Mail the envelope to yourself. Save the unopened letter and when you need a word of encouragement because you are going through a painful situation, open it and

read it. Once you get the Victory, share that experience with someone that may be going through. Remember we overcame by the blood of the lamb and the Word of our testimony (*KJV*, Revelations 12:11).

DAY

17

Everybody Can't Go

Scripture: "For I know the thoughts that I think toward you, saith the Lord, thoughts of peace, and not of evil, to give you an expected end" (*KJV*, Jeremiah 29:11).

Lesson: In life, especially after high school, we form associations with people that are sometimes lasting for the span of our lives, and at other times these associations last for a season or two. Seasons can last for weeks and even years but they have an end date and there is always some lesson we are to take away from it. We must learn the steps needed to be wise and not try to make seasonal people permanent ones in our journey through life. If persons don't have your long-term goals and vision at heart, then you know they are only seasonal. They are only here to help you for the time being. And that help they provide you could be helped on what not to do, and also help as far as what not to look for in a friend. People that have your goals and visions at heart are people who will be there for you long term. They will be the ones that will help support your efforts and will encourage you when you want to quit. They will be there to be your accountability partner when you want to give up or slack off.

Be wise, and choose your crew and associations based on what they bring out in you; not by what they bring you. Just because they feel good to you doesn't mean they're good for you. Yeah, I know we all want a hype crew around us. One that is down for whatever, and will have our backs no matter what. But the truth of the matter is, many of these so-called "crew" members are only around for what they can get. They actually see more potential in you than you see in yourself. And truth be told, if they could trade places with you and have your life, they would do it in a heartbeat.

Please know this; it's not what you attract, it is what you entertain. When you realize your presence is priceless, the foolishness will fall off. Have you stopped to consider that your real issue may be that you're trying to take people with you into your destiny that are NOT supposed to go?

Destiny Work:

❒ Write a list of the five people you primarily surround yourself with. If you aren't sure, just think of it this way;

who are the five people that you spend over 75% of your days and weeks with? These are the people you need to write down on your list.

- ❐ Then put a check beside each person who knows and understands your vision and dreams in life.
- ❐ Next, place another check mark beside those people who hold you accountable for your dreams and goals. These people actually hound you about getting your work done and they act like your parents sometimes when you get off course.
- ❐ Finally, place another check mark beside the people who actually check over your vision and goals that you have listed on paper. Now, if you have people with less than two checks, then you really need to reevaluate your associations with them. They may be in your life for a season, so watch how you allow yourself to be influenced by them.

DAY

18

It's Okay to Grieve

Scripture: "The Lord is near to the brokenhearted and saves the crushed in spirit" (*NASB*, Psalm 34:18).

Lesson: Despite our grandiose imagination of greatness and the pretext of happiness projected on our social media profiles; this life is full of moments of perplexity and profound grief.

When you get the opportunity, research King David and read about his life and how he dealt with situations. King David was very familiar with the process of grief, disappointment, and having a broken heart. I often wonder at funerals why we encourage the families of the deceased loved one to be strong. On the contrary, we should encourage people to grieve. A part of us dies too when someone we love dies. A part of us dies when there is a divorce, when one gets fired from a job, loses a house to foreclosure or bankruptcy, or gets rejected under any circumstances. I am learning that it's ok to grieve.

Allow yourself to move from grief to remorse and then from remorse, we grow into accepting a new norm. My friend, loss is perhaps the hardest part of our shared human experience. What does this process of remorse involve? It involves a truth that everyone we love one day will leave us but there is an underlining of hope.

The hope is that we can escape in our hearts and relive moments. The Apostle Paul expands this truth by introducing us to the *Blessed Hope*, who is Christ Jesus: Titus 2:13 (NASB) declares "while we wait for the blessed hope--the appearing of the glory of our great God and Savior, Jesus Christ". The Blessed Hope is the fact that Jesus is coming back. Death cannot hold you or your loved ones down. We will spend eternity with Christ when he returns. These words are comforting.

Destiny Work:

- ❐ If you have to, cry and cry some more. It's ok to release. Allow yourself an opportunity to be comforted by the Holy Spirit. Meditate on the return of Christ, open your heart the expectations of his performance. Recall the fact that sadness is a part of living but the joy of Christ springs forth like the morning.
- ❐ Be comforted in Jesus name.

DAY

19

Speak and You Will Have It

Scripture: "For verily I say unto you, That whosoever shall say unto this mountain, Be thou removed, and be thou cast into the sea; and shall not doubt in his heart, but shall believe that those things which he saith shall come to pass; he shall have whatsoever he saith" (*KJV*, Mark 11:23)

Lesson: In today's society, people say pretty much what is on their mind. This whole thing of "it's my first amendment right" has really gotten a lot of people in trouble with how they call forth things into existence. Although some phrases are cultural clichés, like "I'm weak" or "I'm dead", etc. when we speak words into the atmosphere long enough, it becomes a part of our subconscious. Then from there what we have spoken gets into our hearts, until it eventually comes into manifestation in the natural. So, we must always remember to say what Jesus has already said about us and about our situations. If we are weak, say I am strong and if we are sick, say I am healed; as God requires us to speak those things which be not as though they were Romans 4:16-22 (KJV). No, you are not telling an untruth or a lie; you are just exercising and demonstrating your faith. God operates in faith and in order to access anything from Christ you must have faith. Watch your words for they will come back to test your faith!

If there are words or things you have spoken over your life and/or to other people, we do have the ability to retract them and renounce them. All you simply have to do is ask Jesus to forgive you of what you said and to retract the statement from happening, as it was done out of ignorance. If you are honest and sincere, Jesus will hear you and He will answer you.

Destiny Work:

- ❒ What are some things that you have said that you need to retract?
- ❒ Make a list and then talk to God about retracting them. Remember, if you write them down, you can be specific in your prayer and confession to God.

DAY

20

If You are not Growing, then You are Dead.

Scripture: "The seed that fell among thorns stands for those who hear, but as they go on their way are choked by life's worries, riches and pleasures, and they do not mature. But the seed on good soil stands for those with a noble and good heart, who hear the Word, retain it, and by persevering produce a crop", (*New International Version (NIV)*, Luke 8:14-15)

Lesson: At least one point in your life, you witnessed someone planting a flower or some type of seed into the ground. If you have never directly witnessed it, I am sure you have seen it done on via a television show or a movie. You may have even had the opportunity to help cultivate the nature of the plant and seed by watering it, fertilizing it, and regularly ensuring that the weeds were kept from growing around it; because you were always told that the weeds would kill the plant as it began to grow. The ground had to be very "good" for growth; meaning the soil, the environment, and just the correct amount of sunlight would help this seed and plant grow to develop into its purpose.

Just as earthly seeds need fertile ground and access to the light of the sun, we as humans need to be planted and have access to a light well. We call this light the Son. Oftentimes as we grow like plants, weeds begin to spring up around us to hinder and block our perspective and perception of the Son. If we as seedlings do not have access to the Son, our spiritual seed could be choked or killed by the weeds (sin) of this world. What are the weeds of this world? Anything that can hinder progress can be considered a weed. Laziness, addictions, procrastinations, etc. can be considered weeds, or blockages to our paths to greatness. It's time to allow the Son to kill the weeds of wickedness in our lives, so that our spiritual seeds can grow into a fertile crop and produce the fruits God has called us to produce

Destiny Work:

- ❒ What weeds are blocking your seed from the Son?
- ❒ Write down a list of things/people that are blocking you from living your best life in Christ Jesus.
- ❒ After you have made this list, start uprooting yourself from these weeds so that you can grow.

DAY

21

The Comforter, Part I

Scripture: "But the Helper, the Holy Spirit, whom the Father will send in My name, He will teach you all things, and bring to your remembrance all that I said to you" (*NASB*, John 14:26).

Lesson: The Holy Spirit is the Mattan (*Hebrew; meaning gift*) of God. As we learned, the Holy Spirit is similar to the engagement ring, the groom gives to his fiancée, which seals the engagement. In biblical times, the engagement or betrothal period required separation to fulfill the obligations of the betrothal and the bridal gift's value was symbolic of the groom's weighty love for his soon-to-be bride and guaranteed he was sure to return to fulfill his promise to wed his bride. The Holy Spirit isn't only God's gift of love and promissory note to the believer, but as John records, He is our Teacher.

At the Last Supper, Christ informs His disciples He would soon leave, but send them another comforter, similar to

Himself. The Holy Ghost would be sent and has come to teach us, the believers, truth. We see this in 1 John 2:27(*New Living Translation* (*NLT*)), "But you have received the Holy Spirit, and he lives within you, so you don't need anyone to teach you what is true. For the Spirit teaches you everything you need to know, and what he teaches is true--it is not a lie...". This is why it's imperative we read/digest scripture because similar to vitamin gummies, they provide the vital nutrients needed for healthy spiritual growth. And it's the Spirit of God that enlarges our thoughts and opens our heart, providing revelation beyond the words on the page, conforming our heart to God's. This is why the psalmist said, "I have hidden your word in my heart, that I might not sin against you." (*NLT*, Psalm 119:11) This is the place we all are growing to; where we are submitted to the work of the Holy Ghost and our hearts come into agreement with both God's will and purpose for our lives.

Destiny Work:

- ❒ The challenge is denying that innate rebellious nature and obediently follow the Holy Spirit. Today, relinquish the need to please self and seek to please God.

DAY

22

The Comforter, Part II

Scripture: "These things I have spoken to you, so that in Me you may have peace. In the world you have tribulation, but take courage; I have overcome the world" (*NASB*, John 16:33)

Lesson: Previously, in verses 5-9, we learn Jesus informs His disciples of His plans to send another Comforter, upon His departure. In the 33rd verse, He shares His purpose for informing them of this and other things is so they would have peace in Him. Peace can be defined as freedom from disquieting or oppressive thoughts or emotions. Previously, Jesus referred to the other Comforter, as the Spirit of Truth. The Holy Spirit not only reveals all things related to Jesus, but demythologizes distortions and reinforces the believer's hope in Christ. The significance of this work of the Holy Spirit is often overlooked because it's one's faith, who is convicted of being inadequate. However, while there is some truth to this, it also points to the disregard for this tremendous function of the Holy Spirit.

Christ said we will be faced with many trials and sorrows, but not to worry because He has overcome the world. In other words, in moments in which doubt and defeated thoughts threaten your joy, it's the Holy Spirit who can remind you that you are more than a conqueror THROUGH Him (*NIV*, Romans 8:37). Though He has the ability to affirm this in you, many of us deny this privilege to sulk in those oppressive thoughts.

Destiny Work:

- ❒ I challenge you to allow the Holy Spirit to have His perfecting work in you. When negative thoughts attempt to attack your mind, be intentional about speaking the words of the Lord over your life, and the peace that surpasses your understanding will guard your heart and your eyes will be opened to the victory that belongs to you through our Lord Jesus Christ!

DAY

23

Delayed, not Denied

Scripture: "Hope deferred makes the heart sick, but a longing fulfilled is a tree of life" (*NIV*, Proverbs 13:12)

Lesson: I want to be transparent with you. Life rarely goes as planned. Like driving I-40, a highway that dips, turns and curves through the Appalachian Mountains, so are the twists and turns of life. These turns sometimes create disappointments and delays. I am not certain what King Solomon was thinking about when he penned these timeless words. I can remember the nights and of agony waiting on an intervention from Heaven. Faith needs a destination of arrival, a purpose; in other words, a manifestation. That manifestation is hope. Faith brings alive what you are hoping for (*Christian Standard Bible (CSB)*, Hebrews 11:1). What are you hoping to come to pass? What is nagging or pulling at your heart? Is it a project or an assignment that is due? Maybe it's a tuition payment or fees for college. You may have received a negative diagnosis. If you can relate to any of these scenarios, I want to empower you. Jesus says, "whatever you ask in my name, that will I do (*NASB*, John 14:13). How bold of a declaration!

A delay is not a denial. The growth process requires the exercising of our faith. Faith is the currency of Heaven and the building blocks of hope. Remember a delay is not a denial. Delays are opportunities to grow your faith and delays act as sifters that separates your will from the will of God. Don't let the circumstances cripple your faith but put your hope in God. Place your uncompromising faith in Him and in the end, you will experience a well-spring of life.

Destiny Work:

- ❒ What is weighing on you?
- ❒ Write a list of your present needs, hopes and desires.
- ❒ Challenge yourself to trust God instead of worrying or growing anxious. Trust the leading of the Lord, and let God lead you on who to talk to about your situation. Allow your prayer to serve as a claim to Heaven, calling on the name of the Lord. My God, I am getting happy just writing this challenge because God's Word is true and He cannot lie. A delay is not a denial. It's only an opportunity to build your spiritual resume and strengthen your faith.

DAY

24

The Spirit of Fear

Scripture: "For the Spirit God gave us does not make us timid, but gives us power, love and self-discipline" (*NIV*, II Timothy 1:7)

Lesson: The world-wide pandemic of the Coronavirus, financial recession and political instability are just a few examples of how life can turn instantly at the drop of a dime. The most seasoned of believers struggle with the temptation to fear. Let me give you a timeless truth, it's ok to be uncertain and still face any situation with courage. Fear is the opposite of faith. Fear paralyzes and causes us to doubt the Word of God.

Will Smith in the movie *After Earth* shared one of the best definitions of fear. He said, fear is NOT real. The only place that fear can exist is in our thoughts of the future. It is the product of our imagination, causing us to fear things that do not exist. That is near insanity. He continues by saying, now don't misunderstand me, danger is very real, but fear is a choice. Wow! Now read it again. God remedies fear by giving us power, love and a sound mind in accordance to II Timothy 1:7(NIV). The next time you appear to be crippled by the tentacles of fear, remember the Word of God and choose faith over fear.

Destiny Work:

- ❒ Reflect on a moment when you were paralyzed with fear. What was the outcome? Take a moment and write an action plan using II Timothy 1:7(NIV) to reinforce your faith in the face of fear.

DAY

25

Beware of the Distractions

Scripture: "For to this end we toil and strive, because we have our hope set on the living God, who is the Savior of all people, especially of those who believe" (*English Standard Version (ESV)*, I Timothy 4:10)

Lesson: Paul kept it real with Timothy. Paul knew that we would get distracted as we seek to live godly in a sinful world. Years ago, I was diagnosed with a disorder, and as a result, distractions are a constant challenge for me. In order for me to remain productive and on task, I have to plan my day and manage interruptions. This may not be your experience, but I believe all of us are tempted to stray away from our primary tasks. The strategy of the enemy is to overwhelm us as believers with choices. As a result, we have to ask the question, what is our strategy against the attacks of the devil?

Let me give you a road map using the Word of God. First,

focus on the Kingdom of God. I saw a meme that says, "decide what kind of life you really want...and then say no to everything that isn't that". Focus is critical. The Word of God says, "But seek ye first the kingdom of God, and his righteousness; and all these things shall be added unto you" (*KJV*, Matthew 6:33). When we focus on envisioning a life built on kingdom principles, the result will be God will add what we need as we mature in Him.

Second, distractions take on different forms. The goal of distractions is to take your attention from JESUS. When we don't have a clear strategy; fear, hopelessness, torpidity, and defeat can simply become the norm.

Third, recognize the weapons of the devil. His weapons are the lust of the eye, the lust of the flesh, and the pride of life (*KJV*, I John 2:16). Don't let what you see cause you to undermine your faith walk. Our perception can be deceptive. Sometimes we have to hold our peace and allow the Holy Spirit to intervene on our behalf. The lust of the flesh is a big one. Your hormones can become your worst enemy. Cold showers are a temporary relief. We need a lasting strategy. Our fleshly tendencies can drive us to sin. Listen! Sex isn't a sin in a godly marriage. Making money is not a sin when you make money ethically and legally. It's not what we desire; it's how we fulfill those desires. Proverbs 16:3(NIV) says, "Commit to the Lord whatever you do, and He will establish your plans. The pride of life merely prefers your will to God's will. Ouch!!! Yes, you are embodying an attitude that wants what you want and wants to do what you want to do, when you want to do it. This is a strategy of the enemy to keep you away from the will of God. We overcome the pride of life by living the prayer stanza, "not my will, but Thine be done" according to Luke 22:42 (KJV).

Remember, our weapons are not carnal but mighty in God for pulling down strongholds (*New King James Version (NKJV)*, II Corinthians 10:4). You can remain on purpose and remain focused even in the most distracting of times. Remember you are a light shining in darkness and a tree planted by rivers of water. Stay focused!

Destiny Work:

- ❐ Write down a vision of the life you want to live.
- ❐ Make a list of the distractions that can keep you away from manifesting that vision.
- ❐ Once you complete writing the vision and listing your distractions, submit what you wrote to God in prayer. Allow God to amend your vision of your life and submit to the Holy Spirit to bring it to the past. In the meantime, continue to fight against distraction and manage interruption. Your destiny is depending on it.

DAY

26

Think Before Posting

Scripture: "A person's words can be life-giving water; words of true wisdom are as refreshing as a bubbling brook" (*New English Translation (NET)*, Proverbs 18:4).

Lesson: Everyone likes to repost rocking memes. Memes are quick, pointed and effective. I wish our lives could fit into 30 characters or less. We all know life is not that simple. Some of the things that are shared online are hilarious, sometimes encouraging but in most cases credulous and downright mean. The Bible teaches us about the power of our words. Proverbs 18:4 (NET) says, "A person's words can be life-giving water; words of true wisdom are as refreshing as a bubbling brook." In short, words are powerful! This doesn't mean that we can't have fun or make light of a moment in person or while online. We should avoid jesting that offends or misrepresents our relationship with Christ. Paul encourages

Timothy, his protégé in the book of Timothy. Don't let anyone look down on you because you are young, but set an example for the believers in speech, in conduct, in love, in faith and in purity (*NIV*, I Timothy 4:12). As believers in Christ, let's be cognizant of our witness. Here is a nugget of wisdom: think before sharing and posting a meme or engaging in a conversation.

Here is an example of a good mental checklist, it's found in Philippians 4:8 (NIV); "Finally, brothers and sisters, whatever is true, whatever is noble, whatever is right, whatever is pure, whatever is lovely, whatever is admirable--if anything is excellent or praiseworthy--think about such things".

Use this checklist as an example before you post:

1. Is what I'm sharing true?
2. Is what I'm sharing noble/righteous?
3. Is what I'm sharing the right thing to do?
4. Is what I'm sharing untainted with evil; innocent: pure in heart?
5. Is what I'm sharing lovely, appealing, adorable, exquisite, sweet, personable?
6. Is what I'm sharing applauding, approving, delightful, enjoying and esteeming?
7. worthy of commendation, praiseworthy and laudable?

I can imagine someone saying, "we can't post anything. Our social media profiles are going to be blank (LOL)". On the contrary, our online profiles can represent the convictions of our faith and our belief in the goodness of God. Humor shouldn't be at someone else expense. Rap artist T.I. once wrote in a song called *My Life Your Entertainment*, "let's avoid drama and remember the world shares whatever, but we share faith, hope, and love". Remember, who and what we represent is always on display. Let's make sure that we display our godly character to the world!

Destiny Work:

- ❒ Take an inventory of your social media profile. Here is a work in assignment: Does my social profile reflect my relationship with Christ?
- ❒ If someone looks at my social profile, what would be their impression of me?
- ❒ Ask a friend to check out your profile and flag post that do not represent your beliefs. Remember, you are the change needed in the world. Your social profile is a witness and is a powerful tool in sharing your faith walk with Christ.

DAY

27

The Spirit of Rejection

Scripture: "For I will restore health to you, and your wounds I will heal, declares the Lord, because they have called you an outcast: 'It is Zion, for whom no one cares" (*ESV*, Jeremiah 30:17)!

Lesson: What is the spirit of rejection? It is the ingrained spiritual, mental and self-construct that undermines one's self worth, and causes a person to reject the Word of God. It is a mindset that says a person is unwanted. This person is unable to properly respond to love from others. This is how rejection is manifested (appears)in a superiority complex, fear, depression, pride, extreme self-reliance, seeking to please others, guilt, feeling not got enough, and shame.

I want to share a very personal moment in my life. I was that kid, odd and not quit a fit to be counted among the popular kids. Where I grew up in the South, children were seen and not heard. This meant that you shouldn't be loud and that you should mind your manners and be very respectful, because this would catch the attention of people. I wasn't the smartest student in the class, but I desperately wanted someone to believe in me. I was the kid passed over, bullied, and ostracized. My situation got so dire that I attempted suicide in the summer of 1992. Unfortunately, my experience is not unique. The spirit of rejection is ruthless, cruel, undiscriminating and downright nasty. It does not discriminate on the basis of race, religion, sexual orientation or religious upbringing.

Maybe you can relate to my experience. If you can, let me encourage you. The spirit of rejection requires deliverance. You can't shout over it, speak in tongues against it or praise your way through it. This demon is different (I know I just messed up somebody's theology).

We also have to remember another thing about this spirit. It doesn't fight fair. It's a cowardly spirit; and it attacks when you are most vulnerable. It attacks when you are unable to protect or defend yourself. It is at this moment that the spirit of rejection tries to take root in your spirit and in your mind.

The spirit of rejection also seeks to destroy your joy of living permanently. It's tough doing anything with a broken heart. I say to you, yes, you are reading this devotion and you are thinking that deliverance can never come your way. You must allow deliverance to be a part of your life so that you can let the healing begin! God promises in his Word, that He will restore health to you, and your wounds I will heal in accordance to Jeremiah 30:17 (KJV).

The antidote against the spirit of rejection is to renew your mind daily. Did you catch that? 365/7/24 (add a rhyme to it and that will flow). You are required to renew your mind daily with the Word of God. Just as a doctor that prescribes medication to a patient, the medicine only works if you follow the instructions and take it. The Word of God says in Romans 12:2 (KJV), "And be not conformed to this world: but be ye transformed by the renewing of your mind, that you may prove what is that good, and acceptable, and perfect, will of God". Your mind can be transformed entirely with the Word of God.

This devotion is not for the faint of heart. Here's an example, the most dangerous person on a basketball team is the player that the opposing team underestimates. You are that underestimated player in this game and God is going to use you for his glory.

I get it, no one can erase the damaging effects of the past but I want to encourage you that God's plan for your life does not include the spirit of rejection. As you seek to fill your mind with the promises, truths, and examples of God's love for you, the gravity of rejection lifts, and you will begin to see yourself as Christ sees you. You are something special to God and don't let anyone tell you otherwise (*KJV*, John 3:16).

Honestly, I am learning not to rehearse, curse or nurse the rejection. I'm not suggesting that we suffer in silence, but I gave myself time to talk about it and then it was time to have a funeral, once buried, I had to walk away.

Yep, bury the divorce.
Bury the one-night stands.
Bury the nasty arguments.
Bury the discrimination.
Bury the job rejection letter.
Bury the bullying.
Bury the isolation.
Bury the depression.

Now, as a result, I can see a harvest of your strength and fortitude. Don't get me wrong, I still have the memory, I choose not to allow it to affect my attitude or thinking. I realize, it's my choice. In closing, rejection hurts but it's not the end of the world. The challenge is to not grow bitter from it but to grow better.

Destiny Work:

- ❒ Using the Word of God write a daily confession that includes God's promises for the believer.
- ❒ Renounce the influence and control of the Spirit of rejection over your life.
- ❒ Reconcile your thoughts and feelings regarding who God says that you are in his holy Word. Remember, God's promise for his people is yes and amen (*CSB*, II Corinthians 1:20).

DAY

28

The Spirit of Offense

Scripture: "Then the Lord said to Cain, "Why are you angry? Why is your face downcast? If you do what is right, will you not be accepted? But if you do not do what is right, sin is crouching at your door; it desires to have you, but you must rule over it" (*NIV*, Genesis 4:6-7)

Lesson: If the murder of Abel took place in the 21st Century, every news outlet would be fighting for an interview. Newspapers would read, ***Murder Outside the Garden of Eden***. Well, it didn't quite happen that way but God in His divine grace gave the most insightful and powerful advice about overcoming the spirit of offense. We will share details about God's advice to Cain later in this devotional, however, let's begin by defining offense. The Oxford dictionary defines offense as an annoyance or resentment brought about by a perceived insult to or disregard for oneself or one's standards or principles. The key Word in this definition is ***perceived***. Have you ever been offended by the words or actions of someone else? How did it make you feel? How did you respond? Offense is the calling card to the spirit of offense. Newsflash!! God does not stop offense from occurring. In fact, Jesus said in Luke 17:1-2 (NIV), "Things that cause people to stumble are bound to come, but woe to anyone through whom they come. It would be better for them to be thrown into the sea with a millstone tied around their neck than to cause one of these little ones to stumble."

Heaven takes offenses very seriously. The spirit of offense is the result of allowing unaddressed actions and words to fester and create disunity. Disunity unhinges the body of Christ. The spirit of offense seeks to cause contention and strife. The deflection of this spirit keeps us from being a support to each other and causes us to become ineffective witnesses to the world. Listen to what the Psalmist said: "Behold, how good and how pleasant it is for brethren to dwell together in unity! It is like the precious ointment upon the head, that ran down upon the beard, even Aaron's beard: that went down to the skirts of his garments; As the dew of Hermon, and as the dew that descended upon the mountains of Zion: for there the Lord commanded the blessing, even life forevermore" (*NIV*, Psalm 133:3).

The spirit of offense grows out of self-righteousness and

vanity. Let's get back to God's advice to Cain. First God asked Cain in Genesis 4:6 (NIV) why was he angry? Ask yourself when you get upset with someone's actions or words, why is this upsetting me? God said to Cain, why is your face downcast? Your facial expressions are a dead giveaway. I am still a work in progress in this area. God already knew what was in Cain's heart but God lovingly and tenderly told Cain, you are wearing your feelings on your sleeves. A sure sign of maturity is learning how to look past a person's initial response and empathize with them.

As growing professionals, your livelihood will depend on how well you respond to others emotions and actions as well as managing your own. God then placed the responsible square at Cain's feet. He said to Cain, if you do what is right, you will be acceptable but if you do not do what is right, sin is crouching like a pouncing predator waiting at your door. The spirit of offense is an ambusher. We overcome the spirit of offense by being prepared and exposing light on its dark and diabolical snare. Let's take God's last piece of advice, He said to Cain, sin desires to have you but you MUST RULE IT. You and only you have authority over how you respond to others. Don't allow the spirit of offense to bait you out of the favor and grace of God. Resist the temptation to get even or to have the final Word, this is the stitch of pride.

In closing, know that offenses will come, maintain your composure, default to doing the right thing even if your actions are perceived by others to be weak and know you alone control your emotions and how you respond to others. When you do this, you expose the crutching predator and take away its power. Remember to hold your peace and let the Lord fight your battle and victory will be yours in Jesus name.

Destiny Work:

- ❒ Take a moment and envision yourself at the top of your profession. What is your plan for dealing with offensive situations?
- ❒ How will you navigate the treacherous waters of dealing with people who have it out for you?
- ❒ What are your values and governing principles?
- ❒ Now ask the Holy Spirit to reveal opportunities where you should have responded differently. Seek to make amends and learn from the moments you didn't represent yourself or Christ in a positive light. Establish a time in your daily confessions that address grace and divine favor in your life.

DAY

29

The Misfit

Scripture: "We are fools for Christ's sake, but you are wise in Christ; we are weak, but you are strong; you are honorable, but we are despised" (*Modern English Version (MEV)*, I Corinthians 4:10)

Lesson: Hello, yes you! It's ok to look around because if you are reading today's devotional this post is going to minister and challenge you. Do you feel like a misfit? I often felt this way because of past experience and hurts; but not anymore. Today, I am a happy Messiah's Misfit. If you feel like a regular misfit, I have some good news for you, you are NOT alone and you are ripe for my recruitment effort. What if I told you that God created you to be a misfit? I was reading the Message Bible and I came across a passage in I Corinthians. It said, We're the Messiah's misfits. You might be sure of yourselves, but we live in the midst of frailties and uncertainties. You might be well-thought-of by others, but we're mostly kicked around. [11] Much of the time we don't have enough to eat, we wear patched and threadbare clothes, we get doors slammed in our faces, [12] and we pick up odd jobs anywhere we can to eke out a living. When they call us names, we say, "God bless you." [13] When they spread rumors about us, we put in a good word for them. We're treated like garbage, potato peelings from the culture's kitchen. And it's not getting any better. [14] I'm not writing all this as a neighborhood scold just to make you feel rotten. I'm writing as a father to you, my children. I love you and want you to grow up well, not spoiled", (*Message Bible*, I Corinthians 4:10-14).

You and I are the Messiah's Misfits. It sounds like a bad girl and guys club, right? It's much better than that. Jesus said in Matthew 16:24 (MEV), "If anyone wishes to come after me, he must deny himself, and take up his cross and follow me." As his misfits, we have committed our lives to following after Jesus; thus, denying ourselves, choosing to suffer for righteousness, and becoming his disciples. So, wear your misfit badge with honor.

Now for the challenge! Put on your seat belts!! As misfits, the closer you get to God, the more you lose. The places you use to go, the people you use to hang out with and things you use to do becomes less appealing to you. As a Messiah's misfit, our challenge is to let things go. The devil tempts us as believers to become entangled with the cares of this world, to become distracted with stuff and our own fame. Remember the life you are trying to gain is not simply achieving a new lifestyle. Lifestyle changes, life does not. Christ said in John 10:10b (KJV), "I am come that they might have life, and that they might have it more abundantly." Oral Roberts once said, "More abundantly" means to have a superabundance of a thing. "Abundant life" refers to life in its abounding fullness of joy and strength for mind, body, and soul. This is the life Christ is offering to all that are willing to follow him. Sign me up for the Messiah Misfits! Keep this in mind, you can't get closer to God and keep your stuff, we exchange our will for his will, our desires for his desires and ultimately, our life for his life. Our submission causes us to allow God to be God in the world.

Lastly, we paint a picture of the life we want but never make the investment in our person to become it. This life will require effort on your part. We can't mature in Christ going through life on autopilot. Our growth in Christ must be measured and it will take a commitment. The Word of God gives us the tools to navigate through this life. As messiah misfits, it's our responsibility to accept the grace God places on our lives to grow our capacity to live holy. If we fail to grow through our submission, our emotions take over and we become superficial and empty. 1 Corinthians 15:58 (NIV) gives our final mantra, "Therefore, my dear brothers and sisters, stand firm. Let nothing move you. Always give yourselves fully to the work of the Lord, because you know that your labor in the Lord is not in vain".

Destiny Work:

- ❐ Let's go back to elementary school. Draw your version of the Messiah's Misfit badge. Think about the symbols you would incorporate in it.
- ❐ What scriptures from the Bible would you use to amplify your witness?
- ❐ Share your drawing with a close friend or family member and once the laughs are over (if your artwork looks like mine) take the opportunity to share with that person what it means to be the Messiah's Misfit. Be the witness God is calling you to be and plant a seed of salvation in someone's life.

DAY

30

God, I'm Angry

Scripture: "Lord, Martha said to Jesus, if you had been here, my brother would not have died," (*NIV*, John 11:21)

Lesson: Martha was hurt and angry. She was hurt that her brother Lazarus had died. She called for Jesus but Jesus delayed his coming for only one reason--He knew God was going to work a miracle. However, Jesus' agenda did not conflict with Martha's expectations.

May I have a moment of transparency? I remember being so angry with God. My marriage was on the rocks, the church I was pastoring was in shambles, my mom got remarried and the people I thought I could lean on betrayed me and all of this happened in a span of six months. I was in debt and I could no longer see the next steps in front of me. Instead of turning to God as my source for guidance, I vividly remember lifting my head towards Heaven and saying "God this is all your fault". For a season, I left the church, walked away from my calling, my wife and got divorced. So, I packed up my car and left town.

I thought that would be the end of my troubles. Honestly for a while, life was grand. I threw myself into my career, time I normally didn't have, due to my ministry obligations was now free. I got pay raise after pay raise, job promotion after job promotion and I was under the spell that I didn't need God. Then reality hit. Boom! I landed in the hospital with four blood clots in my lungs. While lying in the intensive care unit, the Lord spoke to me. He said son, I'm here. I shared with the Lord that I'm still hurt. I'm broken, I'm lost and I'm confused. He said, "son, I never left you. You walked away from me. I'm the source."

I realize at this point that, for me to have a joyful, peaceful, vibrant relationship with God, I must also acknowledge the rage that hindered me. Listen, it was not just annoyance, but rage! I needed to deal with the process of allowing God to be in control. My fellow believer - God can deal with our humanity but now we must learn to accept his divinity.

I'm going to keep it real. It's taken time to cultivate a heart that allows faith to be my proper response. I forgot that even in my anger, God still loved me. Even when I was self-destructive, he still loves me (*KJV*, Romans 5:8). Family listen,

God's desire is to transform us through every experience of our lives. And so, as I struggled, I returned to reflect on God's love. My anger subsided and I realized that everything God allowed to exit my life was for my good. I had to repent and return to God.

Maybe you lost someone you love and you are angry God. I get it. The hurt is real. His ways are mysterious and he sees from eternity. One thing I know about God he understands our pain. I'm learning that it's ok for me to be upset and now I understand, it's not God who I should be angry with. Anger does not work the righteousness of God and anger without a cause is wasted energy (*NIV*, James 1:20). I'm learning through brokenness God is teaching something about us that we cannot see without going through the process. Allow God to give you the grace to work through your anger, resentment, fears and failures as you come to know his love for you.

Destiny Work:

- ❒ Recognize the crippling effects of anger. How has your anger robbed you of the joy of feeling secure in the will of God?
- ❒ Make a list of your grievances. Talk to God about them. Allow the Holy Spirit to minister peace to you as you

decide to submit to the will of God. Trust the process of deliverance, remind yourself that God is faithful.

- ❐ Share your testimony with your pastor and ask him or her to covenant with you as you grow in this area in Jesus' name.

DAY

31

Learn How to Rest

Scripture: "Come with Me by yourselves to a quiet place and get some rest.' So, they went away by themselves in a boat to a solitary place" (*NIV*, Mark 6:31-32).

Lesson: Stress is a silent killer. Stress can cause major illnesses within our bodies to include heart disease, irregular blood flow, panic attacks and possibly even lead to suicide. Believers in the Word of God are not immune to the challenges of living in an artificial work environment that goes against the natural rhythm of life. That's why it's important to bow out gracefully. What does the Word of God say about stress? "Do not be anxious about anything, but in every situation, by prayer and petition, with thanksgiving, present your requests to God. And the peace of God, which transcends all understanding, will guard your hearts and your minds in Christ Jesus" (*NIV*, Philippians 4:6-7).

If the God of the universe took a moment to rest, why won't we? On the 7th day, God RESTED. Jesus' examples this principle when he told his disciples to REST. Prayer and fasting are stress regulators for the believer. It's important to check our motives. It's ok to be competitive but not at the expense or your health, relationship or witness.

The Bible teaches us in Colossians 3:17(NLT), "And whatever you do or say, do it as a representative of the Lord Jesus, giving thanks through him to God the Father". Our motivation and intentions should always point towards God getting the glory.

Be realistic about what you can accomplish in a day. Don't overcrowd your to-do list. Please be aware that stress can cause you to become counterproductive. Maximize your moments to rest and unwind. Turn OFF your cell phone. Disengage from social media and turn off the television. It's ok to not be in the loop for a moment. Your mental sanity requires it. Exercise and eating healthy also plays an important role in stress management. According to I Corinthians 6:19 (NIV), the Bible declares "Do you not know that your bodies are temples of the Holy Spirit, who is in you, whom you have received from God? You are not your own". Taking care of yourself is an act of worship unto the Lord.

Destiny Work:

- ❒ Here is a practical step you can take when you are feeling stressed:

  S - Submit your thoughts to God
  T - Trust He will give you guidance
  R - Reflect how God brought you through
  E - Esteem the Lord above the problem
  S - Seek support from others
  S - Speak the Word of God and stand on His Word.

- ❒ When your life becomes unmanageable, don't fear. Acknowledge it and bow out from all unnecessary activities. Get back to your core values, nurture essential relationships and remember to regulate with prayer and fasting.
- ❒ Finally, take 10 minutes - close your eyes and simply breathe. Be perfectly still. Don't think about what you need to do or what you should be doing, simply rest in the Lord. Think of His goodness and mercy. Feel the cares of your life melt away as you warm yourself to the promises of God. Allow the Holy Spirit to comfort you. Reflect on the above stress acronym.

- [ ] After you complete this activity, plan a date with yourself. Take a day, just for you. Consider it an investment in the temple. Be blessed in Jesus name and remember to rest in Him!

-end-

About the Authors

Min. Ralph Wilson, Jr. is a healthcare administrator for a nationally recognized healthcare system. As the leader of the youth and young adult ministry in the church he and his family attend, Min. Wilson is passionate about seeing young people become born again through Christ and develop an intimate relationship with Him.

Min. Victor Small serves as an associate minister at Joshua Temple Church under Dr. Cedric Walker, Sr. He has a passion for youth and a heart to serve Christ through ministry, the teaching of the gospel, and community activism.

Lorenzo Johnson, Jr., EdD is a current secondary school administrator whose passion is leadership/administration and mentoring youth into becoming productive adults. His heart's desire is to see people develop a love for Christ and to realize their God-given potential and destiny.

Printed in the United States
By Bookmasters